A Christmas Lullaby

Luke 2:1-20 for Children

Written by H. P. Carlson
Illustrated by Susan Morris

ARCH BOOKS
Copyright © 1985 CONCORDIA PUBLISHING HOUSE
3558 S. Jefferson Avenue, St. Louis, MO 63118-3968
Manufactured in the United States of America

All rights reserved. No part of this publication may be reproduced, stored in a retrieval system, or transmitted, in any form or by any means, electronic, mechanical, photocopying, recording, or otherwise, without the prior written permission of Concordia Publishing House.

I had a dream the other night
And I can see it still:
Alone I stood beneath the stars
Upon a windy hill

Outside the town of Bethlehem
Two thousand years ago
As watchful shepherds kept their flocks
Secure within the fold.

A dusty road that wound its way
Into the heart of town
Was packed with hurried travelers
Who came from all around.

I overheard somebody say
That Caesar had a plan
For everyone to go back home,
Each to his native land

So that this mighty Caesar could
Take count of all the world
And order taxes to be paid
By everyone he ruled.

The sounds of night grew gently hushed
Outside the crowded town.
The empty road looked stark and bare
With not a soul around.

Afar off in the distant hills
I saw a lonely pair
Who headed down to Bethlehem
To seek a shelter there.

A woman on a donkey's back,
A man on foot close by—
They finally reached the edge of town
And, weary, walked inside.

They stopped to knock on every door
To find a room within.
How sad, I thought, there wasn't room
At any of the inns.

Joseph was the faithful man,
And Mary was his wife,
Whose time was due for her to bring
A baby into life.

Their beast of burden's frosty breath
Kept pace with weary feet,
As step by step they made their way
Along the friendless street.

But one last knock upon a door
Found help from those within;
"There's a stable out in back
Where you can settle in."

Then, suddenly, a wondrous sight
Before my eyes appeared
As hosts of angels filled the sky
And shepherds shook with fear.

"Be not afraid," an angel said,
"I bring you news of joy;
This night is born the Savior, Lord,
A tiny, infant boy.

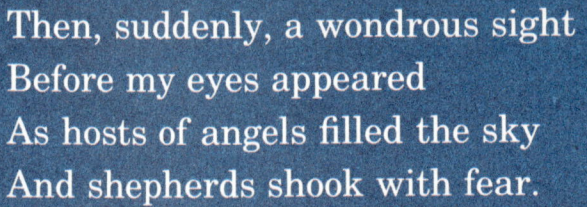

"This babe is lying in a manger
Wrapped in swaddling clothes."
Suddenly a host of angels'
Songs of praise arose:

"Glory to God in the highest;
Peace on earth to men!"
And just as fast as they had come
The angels left again.

Straight away the shepherds headed
Toward the edge of town;
And coming to the stable's door
They one by one knelt down.

Here was Jesus, God's own Son,
For men to magnify.
Then softly did His mother sing
This Christmas lullaby:

"Blest are the eyes that will see Your face;
Blest for all time is this holy place.

"Blest are the ears that will hear Your cry;
Blest are my lips with this lullaby.

"Blest are the hands that will work for You;
Blest are the feet that will follow You.

"Blest are the souls of the innocent;
Blest are the sinners for whom You're sent.

"Blest are the children, the most like You;
Blest are their hearts, full of gratitude.

"Blest is the peace that You bring to earth;
Blest are we all on the night of Your birth."

He truly lived both then and now;
His love remains our peace.
By God's good grace He's made a place
Where joy will never cease

As on that wond'rous silent night
When heaven touched the earth
And made for us a life worthwhile
By His holy birth.

A Christmas Lullaby

H. P. C.   H. P. Carlson

1 Blest are the eyes that will see Your face;
2 Blest are the hands that will work for You;
3 Blest are the chil-dren, the most like You;

Blest for all time is this ho-ly place.
Blest are the feet that will fol-low You.
Blest are their hearts, full of grat-i-tude.

Blest are the ears that will hear Your cry;
Blest are the souls of the in-no-cent;
Blest is the peace that You bring to earth;

1 Blest are my lips with this lul-la-by.
2 Blest are the sin-ners for whom You're sent.

End for stanza 3

3 Blest are we all on the night of Your birth.

From *Second Collection*, by John W. Paquet. Copyright © 1982 by John W. Paquet. Used by permission.